MADLIBS®

HAPPY BIRTHDAY MAD LIBS

By Roger Price and Leonard Stern

PSS!
PRICE STERN SLOAN

PRICE STERN SLOAN
Published by the Penguin Group
Penguin Group (USA) Inc., 375 Hudson Street, New York, New York 10014, USA
Penguin Group (Canada), 90 Eglinton Avenue East, Suite 700, Toronto, Ontario M4P 2Y3,
Canada (a division of Pearson Penguin Canada Inc.)
Penguin Books Ltd., 80 Strand, London WC2R 0RL, England
Penguin Group Ireland, 25 St. Stephen's Green, Dublin 2, Ireland
(a division of Penguin Books Ltd.)
Penguin Group (Australia), 250 Camberwell Road, Camberwell, Victoria 3124, Australia
(a division of Pearson Australia Group Pty. Ltd.)
Penguin Books India Pvt. Ltd., 11 Community Centre, Panchsheel Park,
New Delhi—110 017, India
Penguin Group (NZ), 67 Apollo Drive, Rosedale, North Shore 0632,
New Zealand (a division of Pearson New Zealand Ltd.)
Penguin Books (South Africa) (Pty.) Ltd., 24 Sturdee Avenue,
Rosebank, Johannesburg 2196, South Africa

Penguin Books Ltd., Registered Offices: 80 Strand, London WC2R 0RL, England

Published by Price Stern Sloan, a division of Penguin Young Readers Group,
345 Hudson Street, New York, New York 10014.

ISBN 978-0-8431-3311-0

20 21 22 23 24 25

MAD LIBS®
INSTRUCTIONS

MAD LIBS® is a game for people who don't like games!
It can be played by one, two, three, four, or forty.

• RIDICULOUSLY SIMPLE DIRECTIONS

In this tablet you will find stories containing blank spaces where words are left out. One player, the READER, selects one of these stories. The READER does not tell anyone what the story is about. Instead, he/she asks the other players, the WRITERS, to give him/her words. These words are used to fill in the blank spaces in the story.

• TO PLAY

The READER asks each WRITER in turn to call out a word—an adjective or a noun or whatever the space calls for—and uses them to fill in the blank spaces in the story. The result is a MAD LIBS® game.

When the READER then reads the completed MAD LIBS® game to the other players, they will discover that they have written a story that is fantastic, screamingly funny, shocking, silly, crazy, or just plain dumb—depending upon which words each WRITER called out.

• EXAMPLE (*Before* and *After*)

"_____!" he said _____
　　　　　EXCLAMATION　　　　　　　　　　　　　　ADVERB

as he jumped into his convertible _____ and
　　　　　　　　　　　　　　　　　　　　NOUN

drove off with his _____ wife.
　　　　　　　　　ADJECTIVE

"_____*Ouch*_____!" he said ____*Stupidly*____
　　　EXCLAMATION　　　　　　　　　　　ADVERB

as he jumped into his convertible ____*cat*____ and
　　　　　　　　　　　　　　　　　NOUN

drove off with his ____*brave*____ wife.
　　　　　　　ADJECTIVE

In case you have forgotten what adjectives, adverbs, nouns, and verbs are, here is a quick review:

An ADJECTIVE describes something or somebody. *Lumpy*, *soft*, *ugly*, *messy*, and *short* are adjectives.

An ADVERB tells how something is done. It modifies a verb and usually ends in "ly." *Modestly*, *stupidly*, *greedily*, and *carefully* are adverbs.

A NOUN is the name of a person, place, or thing. *Sidewalk*, *umbrella*, *bridle*, *bathtub*, and *nose* are nouns.

A VERB is an action word. *Run*, *pitch*, *jump*, and *swim* are verbs. Put the verbs in past tense if the directions say PAST TENSE. *Ran*, *pitched*, *jumped*, and *swam* are verbs in the past tense.

When we ask for A PLACE, we mean any sort of place: a country or city (*Spain*, *Cleveland*) or a room (*bathroom*, *kitchen*).

An EXCLAMATION or SILLY WORD is any sort of funny sound, gasp, grunt, or outcry, like *Wow!*, *Ouch!*, *Whomp!*, *Ick!*, and *Gadzooks!*

When we ask for specific words, like a NUMBER, a COLOR, an ANIMAL, or a PART OF THE BODY, we mean a word that is one of those things, like *seven*, *blue*, *horse*, or *head*.

When we ask for a PLURAL, it means more than one. For example, *cat* pluralized is *cats*.

MAD LIBS® is fun to play with friends, but you can also play it by yourself! To begin with, DO NOT look at the story on the page below. Fill in the blanks on this page with the words called for. Then, using the words you have selected, fill in the blank spaces in the story.

Now you've created your own hilarious MAD LIBS® game!

INVITATION TO A BIRTHDAY PARTY

PERSON IN ROOM _____

ADVERB _____

PERSON IN ROOM _____

NUMBER _____

ADVERB _____

SILLY WORD _____

NUMBER _____

NOUN _____

NOUN _____

NOUN _____

ADJECTIVE _____

NOUN _____

NOUN _____

NOUN _____

PLURAL NOUN _____

NOUN _____

ADJECTIVE _____

PLURAL NOUN _____

ADVERB _____

ADVERB _____

Let's Celebrate!

MAD☺LIBS®
INVITATION TO A
BIRTHDAY PARTY

Dear _____,
       PERSON IN ROOM

You are _____ invited to celebrate the birthday
       ADVERB

of _____, who is turning _____
  PERSON IN ROOM   NUMBER

years old! Please arrive _____ at one o'clock on
          ADVERB

Saturday at _____ Palace. Each person will
       SILLY WORD

receive _____ tokens to play games like Whac-
     NUMBER

A-_____, Skee-_____, and
   NOUN   NOUN

_____-ball. Later, a meal of _____ dogs
  NOUN   ADJECTIVE

and _____-burgers will be served. Then we will sing
   NOUN

"Happy _____-day to You" and, after the birthday
    NOUN

_____ blows out the _____,
  NOUN   PLURAL NOUN

we'll eat _____-frosted cake! Presents such as
    NOUN

_____ dolls and video _____
 ADJECTIVE   PLURAL NOUN

are not required but are _____ welcome!
        ADVERB

We _____ hope to see you there!
   ADVERB

MAD LIBS® is fun to play with friends, but you can also play it by yourself! To begin with, DO NOT look at the story on the page below. Fill in the blanks on this page with the words called for. Then, using the words you have selected, fill in the blank spaces in the story.

Now you've created your own hilarious MAD LIBS® game!

ON THE DAY I WAS BORN

ADJECTIVE _____

ADJECTIVE _____

NOUN _____

A PLACE _____

VERB ENDING IN "ING" _____

NOUN _____

VERB (PAST TENSE) _____

NOUN _____

ADJECTIVE _____

NUMBER _____

NUMBER _____

ADJECTIVE _____

NOUN _____

ADJECTIVE _____

ADJECTIVE _____

MAD LIBS®

ON THE DAY I WAS BORN

My mother loves to tell the _____ story of the day
                                ADJECTIVE

I was born. She says it was the most _____ day of
                                      ADJECTIVE

her life. Mom woke up in the middle of the _____,
                                            NOUN

and my dad rushed her to (the) _____. When I was
                                A PLACE

born, I immediately began _____ and crying, and the
                           VERB ENDING IN "ING"

doctor announced, "It's a/an _____!" My parents
                              NOUN

_____ with joy. The doctor wrapped me in a soft
VERB (PAST TENSE)

_____ and handed me to my _____
NOUN   ADJECTIVE

mom. I weighed just _____ pounds and _____
                     NUMBER   NUMBER

ounces. Mom called me her _____ bundle of
                           ADJECTIVE

_____ and said I was the most _____ thing
NOUN   ADJECTIVE

she had ever seen. (But I've seen the pictures, and I think I looked

like a/an _____ blob!)
           ADJECTIVE

From HAPPY BIRTHDAY MAD LIBS® • Copyright © 2008 by Price Stern Sloan, a division of
Penguin Young Readers Group, 345 Hudson Street, New York, NY 10014.

MAD LIBS® is fun to play with friends, but you can also play it by yourself! To begin with, DO NOT look at the story on the page below. Fill in the blanks on this page with the words called for. Then, using the words you have selected, fill in the blank spaces in the story.

Now you've created your own hilarious MAD LIBS® game!

BIRTHDAY PARTY GAMES, PART 1

ADJECTIVE _____

PART OF THE BODY _____

ANIMAL _____

PART OF THE BODY (PLURAL) _____

PART OF THE BODY _____

PART OF THE BODY _____

ADVERB _____

NOUN _____

PLURAL NOUN _____

ADJECTIVE _____

VERB ENDING IN "S" _____

PART OF THE BODY _____

PART OF THE BODY _____

ADVERB _____

NOUN _____

NOUN _____

NOUN _____

NOUN _____

Here is a list of the most _____ birthday party games
ADJECTIVE

and how to play them:

Pin the _____ on the _____: Each person
PART OF THE BODY   ANIMAL

puts a blindfold over his or her _____ and tries to
PART OF THE BODY (PLURAL)

put the donkey's _____ on its _____.
PART OF THE BODY   PART OF THE BODY

Whoever is _____closest, wins!
ADVERB

Duck, Duck, _____: All the _____ sit in
NOUN   PLURAL NOUN

a circle. One _____ person is the fox. He or she
ADJECTIVE

_____ around the circle, tapping each player's
VERB ENDING IN "S"

_____ and saying "duck," over and over. Then, the
PART OF THE BODY

fox taps someone on the _____, saying "goose." The
PART OF THE BODY

goose _____ jumps up and chases the
ADVERB

_____ around the _____, trying to tag
NOUN   NOUN

the fox's _____ before he or she can sit in the goose's
NOUN

_____.
NOUN

MAD LIBS® is fun to play with friends, but you can also play it by yourself! To begin with, DO NOT look at the story on the page below. Fill in the blanks on this page with the words called for. Then, using the words you have selected, fill in the blank spaces in the story.

Now you've created your own hilarious MAD LIBS® game!

BIRTHDAY PARTY GAMES, PART 2

PERSON IN ROOM _____

ADJECTIVE _____

PERSON IN ROOM _____

ADVERB _____

PERSON IN ROOM _____

PART OF THE BODY _____

PLURAL NOUN _____

PLURAL NOUN _____

PLURAL NOUN _____

PLURAL NOUN _____

VERB _____

VERB _____

VERB ENDING IN "ING" _____

VERB ENDING IN "ING" _____

MAD☺LIBS®
BIRTHDAY PARTY GAMES, PART 2

_____ says: One person gets to be Simon. When
<u>PERSON IN ROOM</u>

that person gives _____ directions such as,
<u>ADJECTIVE</u>

"_____ says to clap," everyone _____
<u>PERSON IN ROOM</u>   <u>ADVERB</u>

claps. But if he or she gives a direction without first saying

"_____ says," such as, "Put your hands on your
<u>PERSON IN ROOM</u>

_____," anyone who puts their _____ on
<u>PART OF THE BODY</u>   <u>PLURAL NOUN</u>

their head anyway is out!

Musical _____: Two rows of _____ are
<u>PLURAL NOUN</u>   <u>PLURAL NOUN</u>

lined up back-to-back. There should be one less chair than there are

_____. When the music begins to _____,
<u>PLURAL NOUN</u>   <u>VERB</u>

the players _____ around the chairs. When the music
<u>VERB</u>

stops _____, everyone sits. Whoever is left still
<u>VERB ENDING IN "ING"</u>

_____ is out.
<u>VERB ENDING IN "ING"</u>

MAD LIBS® is fun to play with friends, but you can also play it by yourself! To begin with, DO NOT look at the story on the page below. Fill in the blanks on this page with the words called for. Then, using the words you have selected, fill in the blank spaces in the story.

Now you've created your own hilarious MAD LIBS® game!

HOW TO MAKE A BIRTHDAY CAKE

PLURAL NOUN _____

ADJECTIVE _____

ADVERB _____

NOUN _____

NUMBER _____

ADJECTIVE _____

NUMBER _____

NOUN _____

ADVERB _____

TYPE OF LIQUID _____

TYPE OF LIQUID _____

NOUN _____

NUMBER _____

NOUN _____

SAME NOUN _____

ADJECTIVE _____

COLOR _____

NOUN _____

NOUN _____

MAD LIBS®
HOW TO MAKE A BIRTHDAY CAKE

Preheat oven to 350 _____. In a/an _____
              PLURAL NOUN   ADJECTIVE

bowl, whip one cup of butter _____. Once butter is
                                      ADVERB

soft, gradually add two cups of _____. Then add
                                          NOUN

eggs, _____ at a time, beating until _____.
          NUMBER   ADJECTIVE

Sift in _____ and a quarter cups of all-purpose
              NUMBER

_____. Stir _____ while adding one cup
        NOUN   ADVERB

of _____ and one teaspoon of _____.
      TYPE OF LIQUID   TYPE OF LIQUID

Spoon the batter into a greased _____ and bake for
                                          NOUN

_____ minutes. When the time's up, insert a wooden
        NUMBER

_____ into cake to make sure it's finished. The
        NOUN

_____ should come out looking _____. If it
      SAME NOUN   ADJECTIVE

does not, bake until cake appears golden-_____. Once
                                                  COLOR

the _____ has cooled, frost, add candles, and voilà!—
        NOUN

your birthday _____ is ready to serve!
                      NOUN

From HAPPY BIRTHDAY MAD LIBS® • Copyright © 2008 by Price Stern Sloan, a division of
Penguin Young Readers Group, 345 Hudson Street, New York, NY 10014.

MAD LIBS® is fun to play with friends, but you can also play it by yourself! To begin with, DO NOT look at the story on the page below. Fill in the blanks on this page with the words called for. Then, using the words you have selected, fill in the blank spaces in the story.

Now you've created your own hilarious MAD LIBS® game!

BIRTHDAY WISHES

ADJECTIVE _____

ADJECTIVE _____

NOUN _____

PLURAL NOUN _____

A PLACE _____

PLURAL NOUN _____

ADJECTIVE _____

PLURAL NOUN _____

ADJECTIVE _____

NOUN _____

ADVERB _____

NOUN _____

ADJECTIVE _____

ADJECTIVE _____

NOUN _____

ADJECTIVE _____

MAD LIBS®
BIRTHDAY WISHES

It's my _____ birthday and my _____ friends
          ADJECTIVE   ADJECTIVE

are singing "Happy Birth-_____" to me. But I don't
                                    NOUN

know what to wish for when I blow out the _____!
                                                   PLURAL NOUN

Should I wish for peace in (the) _____ or for a million
                                          A PLACE

_____? The end of _____ hunger or my own
   PLURAL NOUN   ADJECTIVE

personal lifetime supply of _____? I only get one wish,
                                   PLURAL NOUN

so I have to make it a/an _____ one. I can't just wish for
                                  ADJECTIVE

any old _____. But time is running _____!
                NOUN   ADVERB

I know—I just have to ask myself: What's the one _____
                                                          NOUN

I want more than any other _____ gift in the
                                    ADJECTIVE

world? That's it! I'm going to wish for a/an _____
                                                      ADJECTIVE

_____! But, ssh! Don't tell. It's a/an _____
        NOUN   ADJECTIVE

secret!

MAD LIBS® is fun to play with friends, but you can also play it by yourself! To begin with, DO NOT look at the story on the page below. Fill in the blanks on this page with the words called for. Then, using the words you have selected, fill in the blank spaces in the story.

Now you've created your own hilarious MAD LIBS® game!

ODE TO A CUPCAKE

ADJECTIVE _____

NOUN _____

ADJECTIVE _____

PART OF THE BODY _____

NOUN _____

NOUN _____

ADJECTIVE _____

NOUN _____

NOUN _____

VERB _____

ADJECTIVE _____

ADJECTIVE _____

PLURAL NOUN _____

PART OF THE BODY _____

NOUN _____

ADJECTIVE _____

TYPE OF LIQUID _____

ADVERB _____

MAD LIBS®

ODE TO A CUPCAKE

O, _____ cupcake, how I love thee! Let me count the
   ADJECTIVE

ways. Your frosting is as sweet as a summer's _____.
                                              NOUN

Just the _____ thought of you makes my _____
     ADJECTIVE   PART OF THE BODY

water. Whether you are made of vanilla _____ topped
                                          NOUN

with chocolate butter-_____ frosting or made of
                           NOUN

_____ cake with _____-flavored frosting,
   ADJECTIVE   NOUN

it does not make a/an _____ of difference to me. I love
                         NOUN

you no matter how you _____. And, O! There are so
                       VERB

many _____ ways to devour your _____
        ADJECTIVE   ADJECTIVE

deliciousness. One may lick all the _____ off the top
                              PLURAL NOUN

first—or simply shove you into one's _____ in a single
                               PART OF THE BODY

_____. All a person needs is a/an _____
  NOUN   ADJECTIVE

glass of cool _____, and the cupcake experience is
             TYPE OF LIQUID

_____ complete!
  ADVERB

MAD LIBS® is fun to play with friends, but you can also play it by yourself! To begin with, DO NOT look at the story on the page below. Fill in the blanks on this page with the words called for. Then, using the words you have selected, fill in the blank spaces in the story.

Now you've created your own hilarious MAD LIBS® game!

A BIRTHDAY CARD

PERSON IN ROOM _____

ADJECTIVE _____

NOUN _____

NOUN _____

PLURAL NOUN _____

ADJECTIVE _____

PLURAL NOUN _____

ADJECTIVE _____

NOUN _____

NUMBER _____

PLURAL NOUN _____

NUMBER _____

ADJECTIVE _____

NOUN _____

NOUN _____

PLURAL NOUN _____

PERSON IN ROOM (FEMALE) _____

MAD LIBS®

A BIRTHDAY CARD

Dearest _____,
           PERSON IN ROOM

Happy birthday to the most _____ _____ in
                            ADJECTIVE   NOUN

the whole wide _____! I hope all of your _____
                   NOUN   PLURAL NOUN

come true on this _____ day. May your year be filled
                  ADJECTIVE

with joy and _____. I hope you know how proud I am
             PLURAL NOUN

of what a/an _____ young _____ you have
             ADJECTIVE   NOUN

become. I can hardly believe you're turning _____ years
                                        NUMBER

old! My, how the _____ have flown. I have enclosed
                 PLURAL NOUN

a check for _____ dollars. I hope you spend it on
            NUMBER

something that will make you feel _____. Or perhaps
                             ADJECTIVE

you can put it toward that newfangled _____ you've
                                  NOUN

been saving for! Happy birthday, my darling _____!
                                         NOUN

Hugs and _____,
          PLURAL NOUN

Your Aunt _____
         PERSON IN ROOM (FEMALE)

From HAPPY BIRTHDAY MAD LIBS® • Copyright © 2008 by Price Stern Sloan, a division of
Penguin Young Readers Group, 345 Hudson Street, New York, NY 10014.

MAD LIBS® is fun to play with friends, but you can also play it by yourself! To begin with, DO NOT look at the story on the page below. Fill in the blanks on this page with the words called for. Then, using the words you have selected, fill in the blank spaces in the story.

Now you've created your own hilarious MAD LIBS® game!

I WANT, I WANT, I WANT

ADJECTIVE _____

PLURAL NOUN _____

NOUN _____

NOUN _____

NOUN _____

ADJECTIVE _____

A PLACE _____

NUMBER _____

PLURAL NOUN _____

NOUN _____

CELEBRITY _____

CELEBRITY _____

ADJECTIVE _____

ADJECTIVE _____

ADJECTIVE _____

NOUN _____

PLURAL NOUN _____

ADJECTIVE _____

MAD☺LIBS®

I WANT, I WANT, I WANT

The following is a list of _____ things that I would like
                                    ADJECTIVE

for my birthday. Some _____ might call me a spoiled
                            PLURAL NOUN

_____. But like my _____ always says, only
        NOUN   NOUN

the best for his little _____!
                            NOUN

1. A/An _____ pony that I can take for rides to
            ADJECTIVE

   (the) _____
            A PLACE

2. A _____-dollar shopping spree to _____
        NUMBER   PLURAL NOUN

   "R" Us

3. A giant flat-screen plasma _____ that makes TV
                                    NOUN

   stars like _____ appear life-sized
                CELEBRITY

4. Backstage tickets to see _____ live in concert at
                                CELEBRITY

   all of the _____ shows on his/her world tour
                ADJECTIVE

5. A/An _____ robot that does all of my _____
            ADJECTIVE   ADJECTIVE

   chores for me, from cleaning my _____ to
                                        NOUN

   washing the _____. It should do all of my
                    PLURAL NOUN

   _____ homework for me as well.
        ADJECTIVE

MAD LIBS® is fun to play with friends, but you can also play it by yourself! To begin with, DO NOT look at the story on the page below. Fill in the blanks on this page with the words called for. Then, using the words you have selected, fill in the blank spaces in the story.

Now you've created your own hilarious MAD LIBS® game!

GEE, THANKS

NOUN _____

PERSON IN ROOM _____

ADJECTIVE _____

NOUN _____

ADJECTIVE _____

NOUN _____

ADJECTIVE _____

PART OF THE BODY _____

ADJECTIVE _____

NOUN _____

NOUN _____

NOUN _____

SAME PERSON IN ROOM _____

ADJECTIVE _____

VERB ENDING IN "ING" _____

ADJECTIVE _____

PLURAL NOUN _____

MAD LIBS®
GEE, THANKS

So you wanted a brand-new _____ for your birthday,
                                        NOUN

but your friend _____ got you a/an _____
                    PERSON IN ROOM   ADJECTIVE

_____ instead? Bummer! Here is some _____
        NOUN   ADJECTIVE

advice on what to do:

- Don't pout and throw a hissy _____. Keep your
                                        NOUN

  _____ feelings a secret. Instead, put a smile on
        ADJECTIVE

  your _____ and say, "Thank you! I've always
          PART OF THE BODY

  wanted a/an _____ _____!"
                    ADJECTIVE   NOUN

- Check the package for a/an _____ receipt. Then
                                    NOUN

  take the present back to the store and exchange it for

  the _____ you wanted all along. Just don't
          NOUN

  tell _____.
          SAME PERSON IN ROOM

- Give the _____ present a chance. Try
              ADJECTIVE

  _____ with it. You might actually find you
    VERB ENDING IN "ING"

  like it better than any of the other _____
                                              ADJECTIVE

  _____ you received!
        PLURAL NOUN

From HAPPY BIRTHDAY MAD LIBS® • Copyright © 2008 by Price Stern Sloan, a division of
Penguin Young Readers Group, 345 Hudson Street, New York, NY 10014.

MAD LIBS® is fun to play with friends, but you can also play it by yourself! To begin with, DO NOT look at the story on the page below. Fill in the blanks on this page with the words called for. Then, using the words you have selected, fill in the blank spaces in the story.

Now you've created your own hilarious MAD LIBS® game!

SURPRISE!

ADJECTIVE _____

PLURAL NOUN _____

ADJECTIVE _____

ADJECTIVE _____

ADJECTIVE _____

PERSON IN ROOM _____

NOUN _____

ADJECTIVE _____

NOUN _____

NOUN _____

PLURAL NOUN _____

NOUN _____

ADJECTIVE _____

VERB (PAST TENSE) _____

PLURAL NOUN _____

ADVERB _____

NOUN _____

NOUN _____

MAD LIBS®

SURPRISE!

Last year, my _____ friends were planning a surprise
                    ADJECTIVE

birthday party for me. They invited all the _____
                                              PLURAL NOUN

from school—and they accidentally sent a/an _____
                                                ADJECTIVE

invitation to me! I didn't tell my _____ friends
                                      ADJECTIVE

about their mistake. I had a/an _____ plan. The
                                   ADJECTIVE

day of the party, my friend _____ asked me to her
                               PERSON IN ROOM

_____ for dinner. I said yes, but I knew it was just a/an
      NOUN

_____ trick to get me to the surprise _____.
      ADJECTIVE   NOUN

But then I called them from my cell _____ and told
                                       NOUN

them I'd be a few _____ late. Then I quietly snuck
                     PLURAL NOUN

through the _____ door of the house. I saw my
               NOUN

_____ friends hanging out, waiting for me to arrive. Now
      ADJECTIVE

was my chance: I _____ into the room and screamed,
                    VERB (PAST TENSE)

"SURPRISE!" They were scared out of their _____
                                              PLURAL NOUN

—until they started laughing _____. It was the best
                                ADVERB

surprise _____ in the history of the _____!
            NOUN   NOUN

MAD LIBS® is fun to play with friends, but you can also play it by yourself! To begin with, DO NOT look at the story on the page below. Fill in the blanks on this page with the words called for. Then, using the words you have selected, fill in the blank spaces in the story.

Now you've created your own hilarious MAD LIBS® game!

ASTROLOGICAL SIGNS, PART 1

PLURAL NOUN _____

ADJECTIVE _____

NOUN _____

PLURAL NOUN _____

ADJECTIVE _____

NOUN _____

NOUN _____

ADJECTIVE _____

NOUN _____

NOUN _____

PLURAL NOUN _____

PLURAL NOUN _____

ADJECTIVE _____

NOUN _____

ADJECTIVE _____

ADJECTIVE _____

NOUN _____

MAD LIBS®
ASTROLOGICAL SIGNS, PART 1

Some _____ believe that the day you were born
        PLURAL NOUN

determines your _____ personality. See what your
                    ADJECTIVE

astrological _____ says about you:
                NOUN

Aries (Mar. 21–Apr. 19): You face _____ with courage and
                                        PLURAL NOUN

_____ grace. You inspire others with your _____.
ADJECTIVE   NOUN

Taurus (Apr. 20–May 20): Your _____-making abilities
                                    NOUN

are _____. You constantly seek harmony and inner
        ADJECTIVE

_____.
    NOUN

Gemini (May 21–June 20): Your charm and _____
                                                NOUN

usually get you all the _____ you want.
                            PLURAL NOUN

Cancer (June 21–July 22): You easily adapt to difficult and new

_____. You have a/an _____ imagination.
PLURAL NOUN   ADJECTIVE

Leo (July 23–Aug. 22): You love the _____-light. You
                                            NOUN

are faithful and _____.
                    ADJECTIVE

Virgo (Aug. 23–Sept. 22): You are a/an _____
                                                ADJECTIVE

_____-solver.
    NOUN

MAD LIBS® is fun to play with friends, but you can also play it by yourself! To begin with, DO NOT look at the story on the page below. Fill in the blanks on this page with the words called for. Then, using the words you have selected, fill in the blank spaces in the story.

Now you've created your own hilarious MAD LIBS® game!

ASTROLOGICAL SIGNS, PART 2

ADJECTIVE _____

PLURAL NOUN _____

PART OF THE BODY _____

VERB _____

ADJECTIVE _____

ADJECTIVE _____

ADJECTIVE _____

VERB _____

ADJECTIVE _____

ADVERB _____

ADJECTIVE _____

ADJECTIVE _____

NOUN _____

MAD LIBS®
ASTROLOGICAL SIGNS, PART 2

Libra (Sept. 23–Oct. 22): You are honest, energetic, and

_____. You inspire trust in your _____.
ADJECTIVE   PLURAL NOUN

Scorpio (Oct. 23–Nov. 21): Once you put your _____
                                                 PART OF THE BODY

to something, you will not give up until you _____.
                                              VERB

Sagittarius (Nov. 22–Dec. 21): You have a/an _____
                                                  ADJECTIVE

spirit, and you would make a/an _____ teacher.
                                 ADJECTIVE

Capricorn (Dec. 22–Jan. 19): You are patient and _____
                                                       ADJECTIVE

as you _____ toward your goals.
        VERB

Aquarius (Jan. 20–Feb. 18): You are an unusually _____
                                                       ADJECTIVE

and _____ unique individual.
     ADVERB

Pisces (Feb. 19–Mar. 20): You are creative and _____,
                                                     ADJECTIVE

making you a/an _____ artist and _____.
                 ADJECTIVE   NOUN

MAD LIBS® is fun to play with friends, but you can also play it by yourself! To begin with, DO NOT look at the story on the page below. Fill in the blanks on this page with the words called for. Then, using the words you have selected, fill in the blank spaces in the story.

Now you've created your own hilarious MAD LIBS® game!

IT'S MY PARTY, AND I'LL CRY IF I WANT TO

ADJECTIVE _____

VERB ENDING IN "ING" _____

PLURAL NOUN _____

VERB _____

NOUN _____

TYPE OF FOOD _____

PERSON IN ROOM _____

ADJECTIVE _____

NOUN _____

ADJECTIVE _____

NOUN _____

ADJECTIVE _____

NOUN _____

ADJECTIVE _____

PART OF THE BODY _____

COLOR _____

PART OF THE BODY _____

NOUN _____

ADJECTIVE _____

ADJECTIVE _____

Nothing ever goes my way on my _____ birthday. This year
ADJECTIVE

for my birthday party, we were supposed to go _____
VERB ENDING IN "ING"

at the pool. But it rained cats and _____, so we had to
PLURAL NOUN

_____ indoors. Then, I wanted to have a chocolate
VERB

_____ with _____ frosting, but _____
NOUN   TYPE OF FOOD   PERSON IN ROOM

baked me a/an _____ cake with _____ frosting.
ADJECTIVE   NOUN

Gross! And to make matters worse, he/she tripped—and dropped

the _____ cake onto the _____. Then we opened
ADJECTIVE   NOUN

presents. I really wanted a/an _____ _____—
ADJECTIVE   NOUN

but I just got a/an _____ doll. And my dog chewed the
ADJECTIVE

doll's _____ off! Then, I noticed a couple of itchy
PART OF THE BODY

_____ bumps on my _____. I had come down
COLOR   PART OF THE BODY

with the dreaded _____ pox on my birthday! All my
NOUN

_____ friends had to go home. It was the most _____
ADJECTIVE   ADJECTIVE

birthday I've ever had.

MAD LIBS® is fun to play with friends, but you can also play it by yourself! To begin with, DO NOT look at the story on the page below. Fill in the blanks on this page with the words called for. Then, using the words you have selected, fill in the blank spaces in the story.

Now you've created your own hilarious MAD LIBS® game!

BEST BIRTHDAY EVER

NUMBER _____

ADJECTIVE _____

ADJECTIVE _____

ADJECTIVE _____

ADJECTIVE _____

NOUN _____

VERB _____

ADJECTIVE _____

VERB ENDING IN "ING" _____

NOUN _____

PERSON IN ROOM (MALE) _____

PLURAL NOUN _____

PLURAL NOUN _____

ADVERB _____

NUMBER _____

ADJECTIVE _____

VERB ENDING IN "ING" _____

A PLACE _____

VERB _____

MAD LIBS®

BEST BIRTHDAY EVER

The day I turned _____ years old was the best birthday
                        NUMBER

of my _____ life! All of my _____ friends
              ADJECTIVE   ADJECTIVE

and family came to my _____ party. I got all kinds of
                              ADJECTIVE

_____ presents, from a/an _____ that can
      ADJECTIVE   NOUN

_____ at the touch of a/an _____ button to
      VERB   ADJECTIVE

a/an _____ toy _____! Then my wacky Uncle
        VERB ENDING IN "ING"   NOUN

_____ entertained us by juggling _____ and
PERSON IN ROOM (MALE)   PLURAL NOUN

making _____ out of balloons! It was so _____
            PLURAL NOUN   ADVERB

funny! I can't wait until I turn _____ years old this year.
                                        NUMBER

For the _____ party, we're going to go _____
                ADJECTIVE   VERB ENDING IN "ING"

at (the) _____. I can hardly _____!
              A PLACE   VERB

MAD LIBS® is fun to play with friends, but you can also play it by yourself! To begin with, DO NOT look at the story on the page below. Fill in the blanks on this page with the words called for. Then, using the words you have selected, fill in the blank spaces in the story.

Now you've created your own hilarious MAD LIBS® game!

BIRTHDAY BASH

ADJECTIVE _____

ADJECTIVE _____

PLURAL NOUN _____

NOUN _____

ADJECTIVE _____

PERSON IN ROOM _____

VERB ENDING IN "ING" _____

PLURAL NOUN _____

PLURAL NOUN _____

VERB ENDING IN "ING" _____

NUMBER _____

ADJECTIVE _____

TYPE OF FOOD _____

VERB _____

TYPE OF LIQUID _____

PLURAL NOUN _____

NOUN _____

NOUN _____

ADJECTIVE _____

NUMBER _____

MAD☺LIBS®

BIRTHDAY BASH

There are so many _____ options for your _____
ADJECTIVE   ADJECTIVE

birthday party! Here are a few popular _____ to consider:
                                        PLURAL NOUN

Pool Party: Have a cannon-_____ contest to see who
                            NOUN

can make the most _____ splash, or play a game of
                    ADJECTIVE

_____ Polo!
PERSON IN ROOM

Bowling Birthday: Rent a pair of _____ shoes and toss
                                  VERB ENDING IN "ING"

_____ at the pins. Eat lots of bowling-alley _____.
PLURAL NOUN   PLURAL NOUN

Sleepover Celebration: Roll out your _____ bags, watch
                                       VERB ENDING IN "ING"

_____ _____ movies, and eat lots of buttered
NUMBER   ADJECTIVE

pop-_____.
     TYPE OF FOOD

Wet 'n' Wild Birthday: Go to a water park where you can

_____ down _____-slides and jump over
VERB   TYPE OF LIQUID

_____ in the wave pool.
PLURAL NOUN

Putt-Putt Party: Aim for the _____ and hit your
                              NOUN

_____ with the putter. If you're _____, you
NOUN   ADJECTIVE

might get a hole in _____!
                     NUMBER

MAD LIBS® is fun to play with friends, but you can also play it by yourself! To begin with, DO NOT look at the story on the page below. Fill in the blanks on this page with the words called for. Then, using the words you have selected, fill in the blank spaces in the story.

Now you've created your own hilarious MAD LIBS® game!

A SCHOOL-YEAR BIRTHDAY

ADJECTIVE _____

ADJECTIVE _____

PLURAL NOUN _____

NOUN _____

ADJECTIVE _____

ADJECTIVE _____

NOUN _____

ADVERB _____

ADJECTIVE _____

VEHICLE _____

NOUN _____

ADJECTIVE _____

NOUN _____

ADJECTIVE _____

PLURAL NOUN _____

TYPE OF FOOD _____

NOUN _____

MAD LIBS®

A SCHOOL-YEAR BIRTHDAY

Here are some _____ reasons why having your
ADJECTIVE

_____ birthday during the school year rocks:
ADJECTIVE

- You get your birthday broadcast on the morning

  _____ —so every _____ in school
  PLURAL NOUN   NOUN

  knows and can wish you a/an _____ birthday.
  ADJECTIVE

- If your _____ teacher lets you, you can bring
  ADJECTIVE

  in _____-cakes for your entire class to eat
  NOUN

  _____.
  ADVERB

- Your mom or dad can start your _____ day off by
  ADJECTIVE

  driving you to school in the family _____ instead
  VEHICLE

  of making you take the big yellow _____ bus.
  NOUN

- Your _____ friends can sing "Happy _____-
  ADJECTIVE   NOUN

  day To You" over a/an _____ hot lunch of tater
  ADJECTIVE

  _____ and _____ nuggets in the
  PLURAL NOUN   TYPE OF FOOD

  school _____.
  NOUN

From HAPPY BIRTHDAY MAD LIBS® • Copyright © 2008 by Price Stern Sloan, a division of
Penguin Young Readers Group, 345 Hudson Street, New York, NY 10014.

MAD LIBS® is fun to play with friends, but you can also play it by yourself! To begin with, DO NOT look at the story on the page below. Fill in the blanks on this page with the words called for. Then, using the words you have selected, fill in the blank spaces in the story.

Now you've created your own hilarious MAD LIBS® game!

A SUMMER BIRTHDAY

ADJECTIVE _____

ADJECTIVE _____

ADJECTIVE _____

VERB ENDING IN "ING" _____

ADJECTIVE _____

ADJECTIVE _____

ADJECTIVE _____

NOUN _____

ADJECTIVE _____

ADJECTIVE _____

ADVERB _____

ADJECTIVE _____

NOUN _____

MAD☺LIBS®

A SUMMER BIRTHDAY

Having a birthday in the summer also has its _____ perks.

ADJECTIVE

Here are a few of them:

- Since it is hot and _____ in the summer months,

ADJECTIVE

  you can have a/an _____ outdoor party at the

ADJECTIVE

  local _____ pool or even at the _____

VERB ENDING IN "ING" ADJECTIVE

  beach.

- You don't have to worry about taking a/an _____

ADJECTIVE

  quiz or doing any _____ homework on your

ADJECTIVE

  special day.

- Summertime is the perfect time of _____ for

NOUN

  a/an _____ ice-cream cake and a tall glass of

ADJECTIVE

  _____ lemonade.

ADJECTIVE

- You don't have to wait _____ for the weekend

ADVERB

  to arrive before you celebrate with your _____

ADJECTIVE

  friends. In the summer, every _____ is like a

NOUN

  Saturday!

MAD LIBS® is fun to play with friends, but you can also play it by yourself! To begin with, DO NOT look at the story on the page below. Fill in the blanks on this page with the words called for. Then, using the words you have selected, fill in the blank spaces in the story.

Now you've created your own hilarious MAD LIBS® game!

ON MY SPECIAL DAY

PERSON IN ROOM _____

OCCUPATION _____

PERSON IN ROOM _____

NOUN _____

VERB _____

VERB _____

PLURAL NOUN _____

ADJECTIVE _____

PERSON IN ROOM _____

PERSON IN ROOM _____

PLURAL NOUN _____

PLURAL NOUN _____

CELEBRITY _____

CELEBRITY _____

PLURAL NOUN _____

NOUN _____

PERSON IN ROOM _____

A PLACE _____

NOUN _____

A PLACE _____

Happy Birthday!

MAD☺LIBS®

ON MY SPECIAL DAY

The following is a list of historical events that took place on

_____'s birthday:

PERSON IN ROOM

- A/An _____ named _____

           OCCUPATION   PERSON IN ROOM

  invented the _____, forever changing the way

                      NOUN

  humans _____.

                VERB

- Rock 'n' _____ band The _____

               VERB   PLURAL NOUN

  rose to the top of the music charts with their _____

                                    ADJECTIVE

  hit song, "_____."

              PERSON IN ROOM

- _____ broke the record for the most

          PERSON IN ROOM

  _____ eaten in one sitting.

        PLURAL NOUN

- The film *The* _____, starring _____

                PLURAL NOUN   CELEBRITY

  and _____, opened nationwide, smashing box-

         CELEBRITY

  office _____ around the _____.

            PLURAL NOUN   NOUN

- _____, an explorer from (the) _____,

       PERSON IN ROOM   A PLACE

  became the first _____ to ever step foot in (the)

                  NOUN

  _____.

    A PLACE

From HAPPY BIRTHDAY MAD LIBS® • Copyright © 2008 by Price Stern Sloan, a division of
Penguin Young Readers Group, 345 Hudson Street, New York, NY 10014.

MAD LIBS® is fun to play with friends, but you can also play it by yourself! To begin with, DO NOT look at the story on the page below. Fill in the blanks on this page with the words called for. Then, using the words you have selected, fill in the blank spaces in the story.

Now you've created your own hilarious MAD LIBS® game!

BIRTHDAYS AROUND THE WORLD

ADJECTIVE _____

ADJECTIVE _____

NOUN _____

VERB ENDING IN "ING" _____

PLURAL NOUN _____

NOUN _____

PART OF THE BODY _____

NOUN _____

PART OF THE BODY _____

NOUN _____

ADJECTIVE _____

NOUN _____

PLURAL NOUN _____

PLURAL NOUN _____

NOUN _____

ADJECTIVE _____

ADJECTIVE _____

MAD LIBS®
BIRTHDAYS AROUND THE WORLD

People celebrate birthdays differently all over the _____
<u>ADJECTIVE</u>

globe. Here are a few _____ birthday traditions:
<u>ADJECTIVE</u>

Mexico: The birthday _____ takes turns _____
<u>NOUN</u>   <u>VERB ENDING IN "ING"</u>

at a piñata. When it breaks open, all kinds of _____ fall out
<u>PLURAL NOUN</u>

of it!

Brazil: The birthday _____ gets a tug on the _____
<u>NOUN</u>   <u>PART OF THE BODY</u>

for each year he or she has been alive.

Canada: In parts of the country, they celebrate by rubbing butter on

the birthday _____'s _____ so that bad luck will
<u>NOUN</u>   <u>PART OF THE BODY</u>

slip right off him or her.

China: It's customary to have a lunch of boiled _____ and
<u>NOUN</u>

_____ noodle soup. Also, the birthday _____ often
<u>ADJECTIVE</u>   <u>NOUN</u>

receives a red envelope filled with _____.
<u>PLURAL NOUN</u>

Denmark: Birthday _____ are placed around the bed of
<u>PLURAL NOUN</u>

the sleeping birthday _____ and a/an _____ flag is
<u>NOUN</u>   <u>ADJECTIVE</u>

flown outside his or her _____ house.
<u>ADJECTIVE</u>

MAD LIBS® is fun to play with friends, but you can also play it by yourself! To begin with, DO NOT look at the story on the page below. Fill in the blanks on this page with the words called for. Then, using the words you have selected, fill in the blank spaces in the story.

Now you've created your own hilarious MAD LIBS® game!

MY DREAM BIRTHDAY

ADJECTIVE _____

VEHICLE _____

SAME VEHICLE _____

VERB _____

ADJECTIVE _____

ADJECTIVE _____

A PLACE _____

CELEBRITY _____

VERB ENDING IN "ING" _____

A PLACE _____

PERSON IN ROOM _____

ADJECTIVE _____

ADJECTIVE _____

NOUN _____

ADJECTIVE _____

NOUN _____

ADJECTIVE _____

VERB ENDING IN "ING" _____

MAD LIBS®

MY DREAM BIRTHDAY

If I could do anything for my _____ birthday, I'd want to
                                 ADJECTIVE

start the day getting picked up in a fancy stretch _____.
                                                        VEHICLE

But it wouldn't be just any _____—it would be magical!
                              SAME VEHICLE

It would take me anywhere I wanted to _____. First,
                                            VERB

the _____ chauffeur would take me to pick up all of my
      ADJECTIVE

_____ friends. Then we'd go to (the) _____
   ADJECTIVE   A PLACE

and hang out with _____. From there, we'd go on a
                     CELEBRITY

_____ spree at (the) _____. We'd end the
VERB ENDING IN "ING"   A PLACE

day by being magically transported to _____ World,
                                         PERSON IN ROOM

where we'd ride all the _____ rides. This would be
                           ADJECTIVE

followed by a/an _____ fireworks display in honor of my
                    ADJECTIVE

_____. Doesn't it sound too _____ to be true?
   NOUN   ADJECTIVE

Well, it is. And _____ be told, I'm happy spending my
                    NOUN

_____ birthday at home with my family—_____
   ADJECTIVE   VERB ENDING IN "ING"

with them is magical enough for me!

This book is published by

PSS!
PRICE STERN SLOAN

whose other splendid titles include
such literary classics as

The Original #1 Mad Libs®

Sooper Dooper Mad Libs®

Monster Mad Libs®

Son of Mad Libs®

Goofy Mad Libs®

Off-the-Wall Mad Libs®

Christmas Fun Mad Libs®

Vacation Fun Mad Libs®

Camp Daze Mad Libs®

Mad Libs® from Outer Space

Kid Libs Mad Libs®

Grab Bag Mad Libs®

Slam Dunk Mad Libs®

Night of the Living Mad Libs®

Upside Down Mad Libs®

Dinosaur Mad Libs®

Mad Libs® 40th Anniversary

Mad Mad Mad Mad Mad Libs®

Mad Libs® on the Road

Mad Libs® for President

Mad Libs® in Love

Cool Mad Libs®

Haunted Mad Libs®

Prime-Time Mad Libs®

Straight "A" Mad Libs®

Diva Girl Mad Libs®

You've Got Mad Libs®

Graduation Mad Libs®

Winter Games Mad Libs®

Letters from Camp Mad Libs®

Spooky Mad Libs®

Dear Valentine Letters Mad Libs®

Letters to Mom & Dad Mad Libs®

Pirates Mad Libs®

Family Tree Mad Libs®

Christmas Carol Mad Libs®:
Very Merry Songs & Stories

Sleepover Party Mad Libs®

Best of Mad Libs®

Mad Libs® Collector's Edition

and many, many more!
Mad Libs® are available wherever books are sold.